How to be fine about
TURNING
THIRTY

ICE HOUSE BOOKS

Published by Ice House Books

Copyright © 2020 Ice House Books

Illustrated and designed by Kayleigh Hudson
Written and compiled by Zulekhá Afzal & Rebecca Du Pontet

Ice House Books is an imprint of Half Moon Bay Limited
The Ice House, 124 Walcot Street, Bath, BA1 5BG
www.icehousebooks.co.uk

ISBN 978-1-912867-79-0

Printed in China

TO:

FROM:

Welcome to your

THIRTIES!

Where you'll be
twenty-nine for the
next eight years till
you start freaking out about

TURNING 40.

Let us celebrate the occasion
with wine and sweet words.

Plautus

YOU KNOW YOU'RE TURNING THIRTY WHEN ...

Instagram is filled with marathons on a Sunday morning instead of hangovers.

The only invites you get are to weddings and baby showers.

Food shopping is all about the fruit and fibre.

Starting a film at 9pm is too late.

Getting asked for ID is the highlight of your week.

*Everything I know I
learned after I was thirty.*

Georges Clemenceau

Guess it's time to

start that

ADULTING

thing now ...

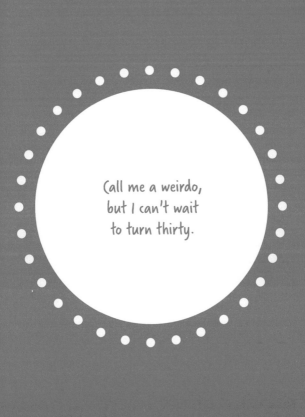

Call me a weirdo,
but I can't wait
to turn thirty.

I'm not thirty, I'm

Our birthdays are feathers
in the broad wing of time.

Jean Paul

BIRTHDAY IDEAS FOR YOUR 30TH

See in the next decade as you mean to go on with a relaxing spa weekend.

Feel the fear and book that skydive or bungee jump you've always wanted to do but kind of dreaded.

Hire a party boat for the afternoon.

Play bubble football where you and your friends are all in Zorbs. Don't forget to look like you're actually enjoying it.

Invite everyone over for a hilarious themed house party.

Old people at weddings always poke me and say **"YOU'RE NEXT"**.

So, I started doing the same at funerals.

*Turning 30 is a
far-off place
in the future until
you wake up and
realise that future is
now your present ...*

is only 12 in Scrabble®.

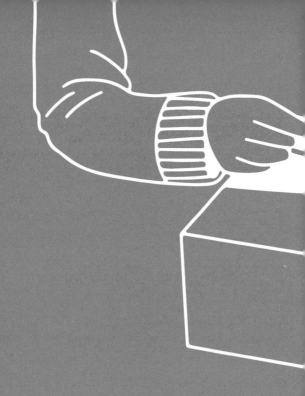

I'm only in it for the presents.

Sea Breeze
Serves 1 | Prep 5 minutes

Ingredients
ice cubes
2 shots vodka
2 shots grapefruit juice
cranberry juice
lime slice for garnish

Method

- Pour the cocktail ingredients (except the garnish) over ice into a tall glass.

- Stir until the glass is cold.

- Garnish with a slice of lime and enjoy your refreshing cocktail!

At age 30,
one receives strength.

The Talmud

You say I'm

THIRTY.

I say you're

JOKING.

PERKS OF TURNING THIRTY

Life becomes more about living in the moment instead of dwelling on regrets from when you were 20-something.

That thing called experience is something you actually have now.

You (hopefully) know who your true friends are.

Staying in to watch your favourite series genuinely makes you happy.

Oh, and let's not forget ... you're not 40!

Goal for my thirties:
keep all my
houseplants alive.

It takes

COURAGE

● ● ● ● ● ● ● ● ● ●

to grow up and
become who you

REALLY ARE.

● ● ● ● ● ● ● ● ● ● ●

E. E. Cummings

Wrinkles should merely indicate
where smiles have been.

Mark Twain

Tom Collins
Serves 1 | Prep 5 minutes

• •

Ingredients
ice cubes
2 shots gin
1 shot sugar syrup
1 shot lemon juice
soda water
lemon slice or twist for garnish

Method

- Pop some ice cubes in a tall glass and pour over the cocktail ingredients (except the garnish).

- Stir then garnish with a lemon slice or twist. Sip away!

• •

The longer I live the
more beautiful life becomes.

Frank Lloyd Wright

Time and tide
wait for no man,
but time always
stands still for
a woman of THIRTY.

Robert Frost

THINGS TO DO WHEN YOU TURN THIRTY

Travel to that place you've been stalking on Instagram.

Try out different types of exercise and find your 'thing'.

Learn to play an instrument. Go on, dig out that guitar you bought 10 years ago.

Learn a new language. Buenos Dias!

Start saving!

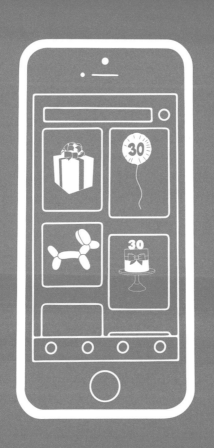

At 30,

you're old enough

to look back,

and young enough

to look forward.

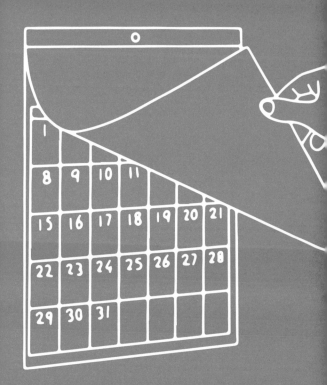

**Many a man who
has known himself at
ten forgets himself
utterly between
ten and thirty.**

Catherine Drinker Bowen

I'm 10,957 days old ...
how about you?

The morning after a night out ...

20s: You GOT this!

30s: ARGH, I ain't got this.

Welcome to your

THIRTIES!

Where your hangover

takes on its own

SEPARATE IDENTITY

and lasts a week.

30's my lucky number.

You're still

WILD AND CRAZY!

(I say to myself as I down a glass of water
and get into bed at 9.30pm.)

I used to think a lot about
my future and career.

It didn't look anything
like THIS future or career ...

I'm going to be
so productive today!

Wastes day watching
TV and napping ...

It took 30 years
to be this
INCREDIBLE.

DINNER PARTY GOALS

So you're turning 30 and it no longer seems acceptable to order in pizzas. Here's how to smash it on the night.

Prep as much as you can beforehand to avoid an 'I'm not old enough to be hosting a dinner party' meltdown on the night.

Go as wild as you like with the details on your dinner party table (if you have one). A centrepiece like flowers or candles works wonders, or failing that, just several carefully arranged bottles of wine.

Keep the menu simple. This isn't the time to try out a brand new recipe with 17 different ingredients and baffling instructions.

Make sure there's plenty of food and drink - as much as your budget will allow!

Most importantly, don't forget to relax, enjoy, and turn off the oven before you go to bed!

Inside every 30-year-old
is a 20-year-old asking,

WHERE DID THAT DECADE GO?

Let us never know what old age is.
Let us know the happiness time
brings, not count the years.

Ausonius

All children,
except one,
grow up.

J. M. Barrie
Peter Pan

Thirty was so **STRANGE** for me. I've really had to come to terms with the fact that I am now a walking and talking **ADULT.**

C. S. Lewis

Here's to turning 30

Where you still feel like
you're 20, until you hang
out with 20-year-olds ...

· ·

... then you're like,
nope, definitely 30.

on a night out in a club at 11pm

Me in my 20s:
I don't want this night to ever end!

Me in my 30s:
Is it still too early to leave?

YOU KNOW YOU'RE TURNING THIRTY WHEN ...

Buying new furniture is
more exciting than new clothes.

If a bar's too loud
you get up and leave.

Time to chill on your
own is pretty great.

An early night never
sounded so good.

Going out doesn't have to mean
you're going 'out-out'. Dinner at
your mum's suits just fine.

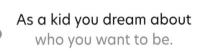

As a kid you dream about
who you want to be.

In your 20s you're figuring out
who that person is.

In your 30s you find
the true you.

Hello, I've finished my free trial of adulting and I'm no longer interested. I'd like to cancel my subscription.

CHEERS TO

You can be

GORGEOUS

at thirty,

• • • • • • • • • • • • • • • • • •

CHARMING

at forty,

• • • • • • • • • • • • • • • • • •

and irresistible for
the rest of

YOUR LIFE.

• • • • • • • • • • • • • •

Coco Chanel

You know

you're in

your 30s

when people

start saying

you look good

for your age ...

DATING IN YOUR 30s

It can be a jungle out there – here's a few tips to help you navigate the evolving world of dating.

Be up for dating someone who isn't your usual 'type'. You never know ...

Have a clearer idea of what you'd like in a partner and don't put up with sh*t!

If you're not feeling it, trust your gut instinct and make like a banana - split.

Keep it real – be your authentic self.

Head out into the real world and try to meet people the old-fashioned way.

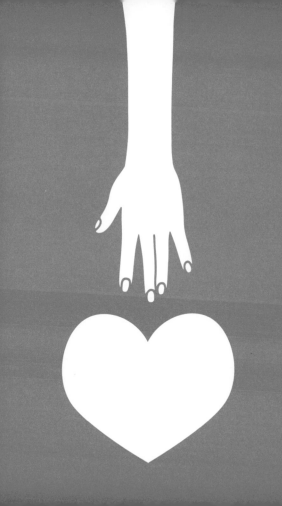

Walking into my thirties like ...

LET'S DO THIS!

The closer I get to 30, the more
I realise my childhood rules
are now my adult goals:

GO TO BED EARLY.

EAT LOTS OF GREEN STUFF.

KEEP EVERYTHING TIDY.

KEEP YOUR COOL

Here's why you should stay chill as f**k about the big 3-0.

If you're not happy with something in your life, there's time to change it.

Ignore the teenager in you that thought you'd be a millionaire with your own island by now. Life has a way of putting you on the right path.

Everyone is winging it, not just you.

You're more secure with yourself, even if it's just a little bit.

Get a grip - you're ONLY 30!!

If opportunity doesn't knock, build a door.

Milton Berle

That moment
when you're
talking about
being a kid
in the 90s
and realise that
wasn't 10 years ago ...

They're not grey hairs.
They're wisdom highlights.

At twenty

years of age

the <u>will</u> reigns;

at thirty

the <u>wit</u>;

and at forty,

the <u>judgement</u>.

Benjamin Franklin

Bloody Mary
Serves 1 | Prep 5 minutes

• •

Ingredients
ice cubes
2 shots vodka
½ shot lemon juice
3 dashes Tabasco®
6 dashes Worcestershire sauce
tomato juice
salt and pepper
lemon slice for garnish
celery stick for garnish

Method

- Add some ice to a tall glass and pour in the vodka, lemon juice, sauces and tomato juice.

- Stir until the glass is cold then season.

• •

- Garnish with a slice of lemon and a celery stick. Enjoy!

Does this mean I have to start separating my **WHITES** from my **DARKS?**

After 30,

a body has a

mind of its own.

Bette Midler

WHEN FOMO BECOMES JOMO

The great thing about turning 20+10 is that when you fancy a chilled one, you just do it. Choose JOMO!

Run a bath with more bubbles than you can handle, just because.

Get in your comfies by 7pm latest with all the snacks and treats you could want within arm's reach.

Drink in hand, pick whichever series or film takes your fancy. Why not watch them all?!

Create a dream board for that holiday you'd love to go on – just think of how much money you're saving right now.

Roll into bed without a head full of regret.

JOMO

(noun)

● ● ● ● ● ● ● ● ● ● ● ● ● ● ● ●

JOY OF MISSING OUT!

Feeling content with staying in and disconnecting as a form of self-care.

● ● ● ● ● ● ● ● ● ● ● ● ● ● ● ●

Antonym: FOMO

You are

only young

once, but

you can stay

immature

indefinitely.

Ogden Nash

Welcome to your

THIRTIES!

. . . .

When you're the youth of
OLD AGE.

DON'T WORRY!

You'll be used to being in your thirties by the time you turn **FORTY.**

There is nothing
permanent except change.

Heraclitus of Ephesus

FIVE THINGS YOU SHOULD WEAR IN YOUR 30s

Whatever you want.

Whatever you want.

Whatever you want.

Whatever you want.

And, oh ... whatever you want!

You are never too old to set another
goal or to dream a new dream.

C. S. Lewis

Here's to turning 30
and giving less

SH★TS

Cucumber Collins
Serves 1 | Prep 5 minutes

• •

Ingredients
⅓ medium cucumber, peeled
½ shot lemon juice
ice cubes
soda water
cucumber slice for garnish

Method

- Purée the cucumber in a food processor. Add the puréed cucumber and lemon juice to a cocktail shaker. Shake well.

- Pour the cucumber and lemon mixture into a glass over ice. Top with the soda water and garnish with a slice of cucumber.

• •

- Sit back and relax with a mocktail that'll leave you feeling refreshed instead of messed (up).

Party like you're seventeen!

Regret it in the morning ...

The only time you really live
is from thirty to sixty.

The young are slaves to dreams;

the old to regrets.

Only the middle-aged
have all their five senses
in the keeping of their wits.

Theodore Roosevelt

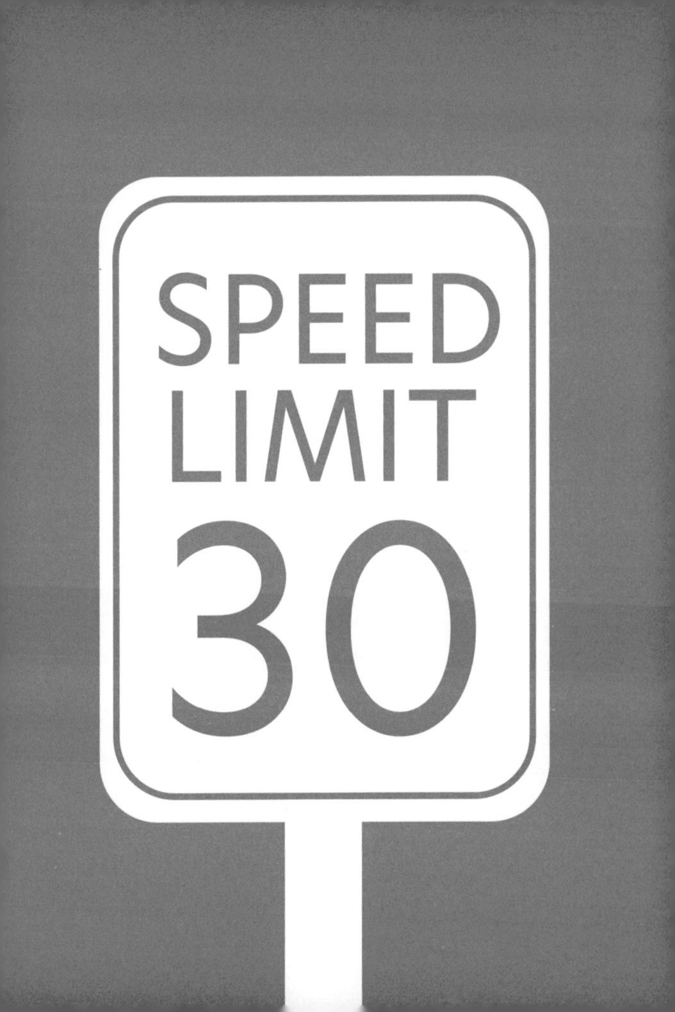
SPEED
LIMIT
30

Celebrate your

THIRTIES!

• • • • • • • • • • • • • • • • • • •

You have an
AWESOME
ride ahead of you.